Copyright © 2020 Rezwana Derbyshire and Doug Derbyshire

All rights reserved. No part of this book may be reproduced
or used in any manner without the prior written permission of the copyright owner,
except for the use of brief quotations in a book review.

To request permissions, contact the publisher at Admin@ TellTheKids.com.

Hardback ISBN: 978-1-953935-01-4
Paperback ISBN: 978-1-953935-00-7
Ebook ISBN: 978-1-953935-02-1

First edition October 2020.

Author Rezwana Derbyshire
As told by Doug Derbyshire
Edited by Diane Hamilton
Cover art by Jerry and Faith McCollough
Layout Design by Nick Zink
Illustrations by Jerry and Faith McCollough

Printed by Ingram Spark in the USA.
Published by
Tell The Kids, LLC
Fort Worth, TX

TellTheKids.com

To our children and our children's children for generations to come.

It was Christmas Day in a land far away
Such a day there never would be,

For the tale of this day is still told today
It's amazing, stay tuned and you'll see!

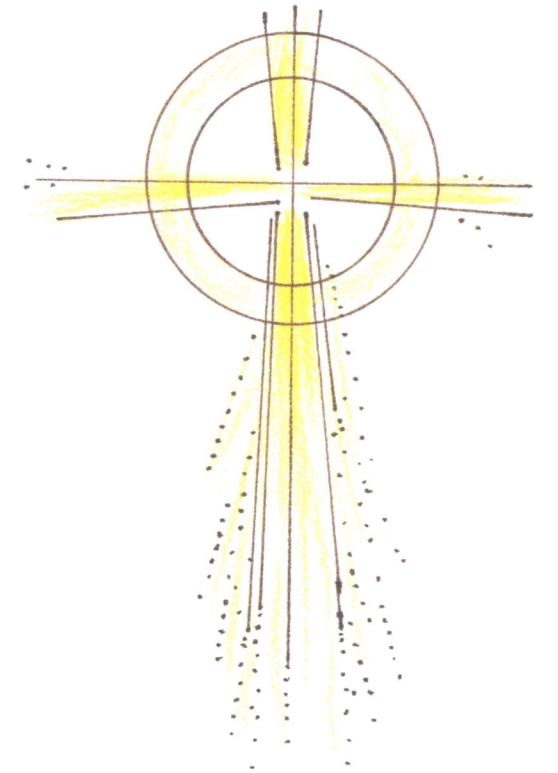

Every year with joy and great cheer
The story of Jesus was told,

The townspeople gathered with wishing and wonder
And watched the story unfold.

An idea came to a Doctor and wife
To make this Christmas Day grand,
Their hope was to make the tale come alive
So they called Mr. Elephant Man.

Mr. Elephant Man and his big bellied beast
Walked into the Doctor's front yard,

"It needs to eat fruit, two barrels at least!"
"No problem! That shouldn't be hard."

The Doctor arranged for the fruit to be brought
"This should be enough, I think!"

To his shock and surprise the elephant ate
ALL the fruit in a flash and a blink!

"Oh dear," thought the Doctor as he started to wonder
How much trouble this beast would be,
As a hesitant client of this insatiable giant
He would just have to wait and see.

With snack time now over there was work to be done
The elephant bowed down low,
And on climbed the Doctor's beautiful wife
"Into the town we go!"

So they rode into town with great style and fashion
Inviting the people they met,

"Come to our house this Christmas night!
It's a night you will never forget!"

They came back to the house, the first job done
And as soon as they came through the gate,
"Elephant hungry!" Sang Mr. Elephant Man
"But the elephant only just ate!"

The elephant sniffed as it caught a big WHIFF
Of bananas from somewhere nearby,
It grabbed a tree trunk and gave it a tug
It clearly would not be denied.

And out with a RIP the tree left the ground
The elephant stuffed its big mouth,
The Doc and his wife stood with jaws open wide
Their plan they quickly did doubt!

The Doc and his wife got word from a friend
"Five hundred are coming tonight!"
"What an answer to prayer that many will come!
May the story of Jesus shine bright!"

Mr. Elephant Man and pachyderm pet
Approached with another request,
"Now it wants water," Mr. Elephant Man said
"Banana is hard to digest."

The answer was simple this need could be met
So the Doctor walked up to the hose,
With a great sputter, out came the water
And sprang up near the elephant's nose.

For a short spell of time all things seemed fine
The elephant peacefully drank,
Then it suddenly changed its elephant mind
And gave the hose a big yank!

It pulled and it ripped and it tore and it tugged
As pipes shot out of the ground,
Water was bubbling all over the yard
And made a peculiar sound!

The wreckage was huge, the plumbing laid bare
But the elephant wasn't quite done,
A pipe flew out from inside the house
The Doc and his wife were both stunned!

The Doc closed his eyes and took a deep breath
And wondered what Jesus would do,
Was it worth all the trouble to bring the beast here
And turn his home into a zoo?

He brushed off his fears and set his mind back
To the task that was looming ahead,
He dressed like a wise man, climbed on to the beast
And prayed it would do as he said.

The night quickly came, the music was playing
It was time for the show to begin,
The townspeople sat with great expectation
Every possible spot was filled in.

The moment was here the Doc and the beast
Strode onto the manger scene,
The elephant went above and beyond
And that was quite unforeseen!

Just like the Doctor, in wise man garb
The elephant got down on one knee,
He worshipped the babe
                Who lay in the manger
                Who came to set us all free.

Who would have thought that this troublesome titan
Who'd had a disastrous day,
Would be the right choice when it mattered the most
It would do so much more than obey.

With a heart full of praise (and a tinge of relief)
Doc shared the Good News with them all,

"God sent His own Son to die for our sins,
Who will now answer His call?"

A tiny Thai woman from far in the back
Stood up and made herself known,

"I see what God did to rid me of sin.
I want to make God my own!"

Right there in the presence of all of the town
She prayed and was wonderfully changed,
Leaving behind the life she once knew
Her allegiance to Jesus made plain.

The show now concluded, the townspeople left
Oh, what a tumultuous day!
It started with trouble and ruin and wreckage
But the end was more than okay.

The Doctor reflected on what the Lord did
And He answered the question he had,

"Is it worth it to have big ideas for God
When it seems the ideas are bad?"

---

His house was a wreck, he had no running water
And all the banana trees gone,
The meddlesome mammoth had done enough damage
To his beautiful manicured lawn.

But the Doctor had peace in his heart that night
As under the covers he curled,
One life changed and surrendered to Jesus
Is worth all the strife in the world.

# Tell The Kids...

This true story of the Christmas elephant is wonderful to tell and retell because on that day a woman (her name was Mrs. P) was born-again. She heard the story of Jesus' birth and how He died on the cross for her and she immediately put her trust in Him and asked Him to take away her sin.

In the Bible, Jesus, God's Son, said that everyone must be "born again." So Doug and Cheryl went to Thailand as missionaries to tell people who had never heard of Jesus, how they can be born-again.

To be born-again, like the woman in the story, we must believe that God made the world – the world did not form by itself. We must recognize that God is perfectly without sin, and He made us to be perfectly without sin too. But we have sinned, and we do sin and that ruins our relationship with Him. Taking away sin is very hard. The punishment for sin is death. But with great love, Jesus died for us! Then, after dying, Jesus came back to life! And if we will turn from our sin and ask Jesus to forgive us, He will forgive us and make us like we had been "born again."

**If you want to be Born-Again, you can pray right now:**

- Pray and tell God that you believe that He made the world.

- Tell God that you believe He is holy and perfect and confess to Him that you are not.

- Thank God for His love and thank Him that His Son Jesus came to take away our sins by dying for us on the cross.

- Ask Him to cleanse you of all your sins, and tell Him your commitment to live to honor Him from this day on.

Years ago, Mrs. P prayed like this after watching the Christmas elephant, and she lived to honor Jesus from that day forward. May the story of the Christmas elephant inspire all of us to honor Jesus from this day and forever.

-Dr. Doug Derbyshire

All proceeds from this book will go to help Thai Country Trim women's ministries in Thailand. Thai Country Trim makes Christmas ornaments that are sold all over the world.
Since the pandemic of COVID19 their sales came to an abrupt halt. They had to furlough over three hundred rural Thai women who had no other means of income.

If you would like to order our Christmas elephant ornament to go along with your book you can find it in our Etsy shop.

https://www.etsy.com/shop/ThaiCountryTrim

www.ingramcontent.com/pod-product-compliance
Lightning Source LLC
Chambersburg PA
CBHW041915230426

43673CB00016B/414